Change Your Questions

CHANGE YOUR CHURCH

HOW TO LEAD WITH POWERFUL QUESTIONS

J. Val Hastings, MCC

Phone: 610-385-8034

Email: val@coaching4clergy.com

Web Site: www.coaching4clergy.com

ISBN #978-0-9886128-1-5

Advance Praise for
Change Your Questions, Change Your Church

When I first met Val Hastings, it was as a pastor who was required to have a coach by the presiding bishop. I said yes reluctantly because I was willing to do anything needed to step into the position God was calling me to. I was not at all sure of what coaching would look like in this new setting or how it would help. The only coaching I had ever received was connected to sports and I knew that was nothing like what this would be like. So, I stepped into what would become a magnificent relationship with Val that has lasted for more than five years, with coaching at various levels over those five years.

During those years of coaching, the questions that Val asked me allowed me to peel back the layers of confusion and the walls of defense to get at the core issues at hand. I can say with certainty that it is the questions asked, more than any answers given, that made and continue to make, our coaching sessions worthwhile and transformational. The first question that rocked my world was a simple one. While discussing a more than busy day and a personal need to be involved in everything, Val asked me, "What is it that only you can do?" I had never considered that before and the questions stopped me fast in my tracks.

That's what the right questions can do. They have the ability to open doors for exploration that can reveal what is at the heart of a personal, corporate or congregational matter. The right question has the ability to tilt one's head just slightly enough so that new realities can be seen. The right questions can stop mental traffic that is stuck, or exit our thoughts off the busy pace of life and onto the back roads of introspection. That's why I believe this book is necessary for pastors and leaders today. There is so much going on and each leader finds him- or herself from time to time needing to get off the bus and consider what is going on in new and different ways.

The toughest question Val ever asked me as he was coaching me into new places was, "So, what are you afraid of?" It was a question that still makes me shiver when I hear it. It's also a question that I've asked people I am coaching. It was the right question at the time and it revealed feelings that I needed to deal with, if I was going to be the pastoral leader I needed to be and that God was calling me to be.

Val offers church leaders a wonderful approach to moving through roadblocks, addressing staffing issues, dealing with a stuck church, working out a mission and vision plan for the future, and so much more. At the church where I'm pastoring, we have adopted a coaching model for all of our ministry leaders. By asking the right questions, people in ministry feel listened to for the first time. Leaders feel valued and creativity is encouraged by simply listening and asking the right questions. Ministry servants feel assured that they will not be stuck in a volunteer position beyond their limits, because coaching questions will be used on a regular basis to evaluate and challenge people about how they are serving.

I don't want to make this sound overly simplistic. It's taken us years to develop our coaching abilities as pastoral leaders so that it happens more like second nature. We stumbled at first and there were times when we asked all the wrong questions and got all the wrong feedback. Val addresses just those kinds of situations and frustrations in this very helpful book. His clear and concise listing of steps that can be taken, the kinds of questions to be asked and how to reframe your current questions, and examples of how others maneuvered the coaching waters provide an easy guide for any leader facing any challenge.

Pastors, ministry leaders, church staffs, church boards/ councils and ministry servants will all benefit from learning a coaching style of leadership. The transition from an old model of church leadership to a coaching model is made easier when you begin to understand what the right questions are, how to ask them, and when to ask them of the leaders of your church.

Let me say this – pay close attention to the cautions that Val lays out in this book. Take these steps slowly and make sure you take time to process your journey from time to time. This process is more than rewarding when people see what you're doing, but it is equally frustrating when coaching is done in the wrong spirit. Make sure you're asking yourself the right questions, and perhaps be open to being coached, as you are learning how to change the church into a place where coaching is the norm for ministry and success.

Coaching is a bold move, but worth the work it takes when you see people excited about ministry and your church taking off in new directions. Val helps by clarifying the importance of the right questions. So, what's keeping you from taking your church to the next level … it just might be the right questions. By reading *Change Your Questions, Change Your Church*, you're on your way to the change God has in store for you and the entire congregation.

David Biser
Vision Pastor
CrossPoint Church
Harrisburg, PA

Acknowledgements

I am one of the lucky ones!

I am one of those individuals who has been surrounded by people that bring out the best in me. This book is dedicated to those who have empowered me as a person, a pastor and a professional coach.

I grew up with parents that encouraged me to pursue my dreams – and to dream big. I remember, as a child, telling them that I wanted to be a farmer, fireman, professional athlete, astronaut and pastor. And they told me to go for it. Thank you, Mom and Dad, for the years of encouragement that you have offered me.

My wife, Wendy, continually encourages me to pursue my dreams! How great to have a partner who wants the best for me. Thank you for your support and encouragement. What a gift you have given me.

To my two daughters, Bryanna and Shelby, you are my source of pride and joy. It's great being your Dad and helping you dream big and live out your dreams.

We've got a great team and faculty at Coaching4Clergy. I appreciate your commitment to our global vision and your contributions to this book.

To my Online Business Manager and Virtual Assistant, Laura Pumo, and her team at Office DEVA, thank you for pulling this all together for me. Your assistance was invaluable.

To my editor, Linda Dessau, thank you for bringing my ideas to light and helping me clarify and polish my message. Working with you was one of the best decisions I ever made with my business.

To all of the pastors, ministry staff and church leaders that I have coached and trained, this book is filled with what you have taught me. Others will benefit from you.

Contents

"If I had an hour to solve a problem and my life depended on the answer, I would spend the first 55 minutes figuring out the proper questions to ask. For if I knew the proper questions, I could solve the problem in less than 5 minutes."

— *Albert Einstein*

SECTION ONE

How History Changed on a Single Question

On my recent travels to deliver a coach training program, I heard a statement on the radio that stopped me cold: History changed when a single question changed; when we stopped asking, "How do we get to the water?" and started asking, "How do we get the water to us?"

What a radical shift for us as human beings!

My thoughts went immediately to how this relates to us in ministry. How would our churches change if we were to change our questions?

For example, here are three of the questions you might be asking now:

Question #1: How do we get "them" to come to us?

Boards and leaders literally spend hours on this question, but I think that if we change that question, we could produce entirely different outcomes. What if we ask, "How can we go to them?" Or, we could ask, "How can we have a positive impact on our community-at-large?"

In a promotion for his new book, *Focus*, Lovett H. Weems, Jr., suggests another question for us to reflect on: "If the percentage of married couples with young children has declined by half since the 1950s, why is that still the group we focus most on reaching?"

Question #2: How much longer can we afford a full-time pastor?

This question suggests scarcity thinking – focusing on what's lacking instead of what's abundant. What if we ask, "What more can we do with the resources we have?" Or, "How can we develop the people we have so they can make a bigger contribution and everyone wins?"

Question #3: How do we get people to fund our budget?

This sounds like we're trying to cajole or even manipulate people into doing something they don't really want to do. What if we ask, "What are people most excited about, and how can we give them the opportunity to support us while fulfilling their own interests and passions?" People are happy to invest time, energy and resources when it is also satisfying to them.

Now is the time to examine the questions that you and your church are asking. Are they limiting, like our examples above, or are they powerful? And, what's the difference?

By the time our predecessors had reframed their question about water, they already had the technology to bring the water to them. The times were right, the changes were underway. Well, today we are in another period of change.

Everyone is feeling it. In August 2010, Eugene Cho published a blog post called "Death by Ministry" that included some alarming statistics about how so many pastors today are feeling burnt out, underappreciated and alone.

In *Liberating Hope: Daring to Renew the Mainline Church,* authors Michael S. Piazza and Cameron B. Trimble reference author Anne Rice's July 2010 Facebook page comment where she said she "quit being a Christian" because she refuses to be insensitive to those who are different. They tell of the huge outpouring of support for her sentiments – 3,600+ people who clicked to "like" the post and 1,800+ who wrote comments. "Anne Rice gave voice to what a lot of people were thinking," write Piazza and Trimble, "They loved Jesus but they'd lost faith in the church."

A report called "A Decade of Change in American Congregations 2000-2010" (*Faith Communities Today*) revealed that, in 2010, more than one in four congregations had fewer than 50 people in the pews.

The report was authored by David A. Rozen, who conducted a series of studies between 2000 and 2010, with survey responses culled from more than 28,000 randomly sampled congregations. Another alarming – but not surprising – detail from the study was the high percentage of congregants who are 65 years or older. As Rozen points out, "Half of the congregations could lose one-third of their members in 15 years."

In *The Present Future,* Reggie McNeal points to a similar concern from a financial angle. He says that the current church culture in North America is at risk of dying off completely, with 80% of church money contributions coming from people aged 55 and older. He goes on to point out that, while affiliation with institutional religion is down, interest in spirituality is up.

With this high level of interest in spirituality in North America, church membership and attendance (your church included) are at a record low. Pastors are dispensing information that the spiritually curious have no interest in. They lecture about what people should do, instead of inviting people into a deeper place of exploration, instead of listening with an open mind and open heart.

This book is about reframing your questions in order to change your church. Reggie McNeal also invites us to reframe in his article, *Fast Forwarding Your Church's Community Engagement*. He sees us being called to join a movement of the Spirit, noting that "God seems to be having a different conversation with the church about its role in the world."

He suggests that "missional ministry requires a different scorecard than churches have used in the past." He asks churches to measure their missionary activities outside the church, rather than their numbers inside the church.

Far from being the end of the story, I believe this is a new beginning; that we're on the cusp of the next great reawakening of ministry.

How is this like other transformational moments in history?

- Consider how on a snowy January 20, 1961, John F. Kennedy mobilized the American people by suggesting the refrain, "Ask not what your country can do for you – ask what you can do for your country."

- Consider how the fate of the Jewish people was forever changed when God implored Moses to reframe his questions of doubt and fear in order to believe, "I am enough." And he was.

My own personal history changed immeasurably on the day that my mentor coach reframed my question, "I'm just Val, how can I do all of that?" with the question, "What if being just Val is exactly what's called for in this situation?"

Being just Val, I've been honored to be at the forefront of a movement that is having a ripple effect through churches, congregations and communities all over the world. Ten years ago, I had to explain what coaching is. Today, there are pastors and church leaders clamoring to learn and master coaching skills and apply them in ministry.

And it all starts with questions.

"Effective leadership is not a luxury, but a necessity."
— J. Val Hastings

"Most leaders don't need to learn what to do. They need to learn what to stop." – Peter Drucker

SECTION TWO

What are Powerful Questions?

One of a leader's greatest tools is powerful questions. At a time when the ministry platelets are shifting, it is powerful questions that will help leaders and churches to navigate forward. Coaching with powerful questions has proven to be very effective in helping individuals and groups get unstuck, and it can do the same in the local church and various ministry settings.

Brett had been at his current church for over 25 years. During our coaching session he said, "I'm dreading our upcoming mission development retreat." Upon further inquiry, I discovered that every five years, whether they needed it or not, his church held a mission development retreat to come up with their new mission. As their long-term pastor, Brett knew the drill. In frustration, Brett asked, "Why do we have to keep coming up with a new mission? What if we became a people 'in mission'?"

Brett wasn't questioning the value of being clear about their church's mission. But what Brett had just articulated was a whole new way of being – a culture change. Now, instead of "What's our new mission?", Brett was prepared to raise an entirely different, transformation question, "How do we become a people in mission?" P.S. During the retreat, Brett reported that there was a church-wide sigh of relief when Brett reframed the question. Everyone was ready to shift the question.

Powerful questions are usually open-ended, leaving room for contemplation and reflection, instead of being limited to yes or no, or specific choices. Powerful questions promote the exploration of new possibilities, stimulate creativity and put the respondents in a place of responsibility. They empower individuals and groups to consider what is right for them.

During a recent Coaching4Clergy faculty call, we were discussing powerful questions, when Larry Ousley made the following observation:

> *Powerful questions come with the assumption of an expectation of choice and possibility. When we as coaches ask powerful questions, we are standing in the place of "there is hope, there is choice, there is opportunity for change." We are living in that assumption with the client and helping them move toward this place rather than a stuck place. So, our way of being as we express powerful questions is from this stance of choice and possibility. We would not ask powerful questions if we weren't standing in a place of hope. There would be no purpose in asking powerful questions if there were not the possibility of new awareness and new perspectives leading toward action. As coaches, we ground this assumption in our way of being, as we hold the space and ask powerful questions.*

Powerful questions open us to possibilities beyond the reality that's in front of us today, stretching us into the territory of our visions to ask, "What is God's invitation for us in this situation today?"

> *"We don't have any children or youth at our church on Sunday mornings. How can we compete with the other*

churches in town? What will it take to fill up our Sunday morning classes again?" The church asking these questions was made up of people primarily 65 years or older. Their children and grandchildren had grown up in this church and moved on. They desperately wanted to fill their Sunday programs with children and youth.

Their church coach asked them, "What are the unique opportunities for kids at your church right now?" The group couldn't come up with any answers. "Okay," the coach finally said, "Never mind Sundays. What are some opportunities for kids to be at your church on the other days of the week?" They agreed to ponder that question on their own.

A few weeks later, the coach returned for a follow-up session. To his surprise, the church members reported: "You know, we need to stop trying to be like other churches on Sunday. That's just not us – at least not right now. On Sunday, we're church just like we've been for the past 50+ years. That's not going change in the near future. But we can be different from Monday to Friday. Most of us are retired and the community really needs an after-school program with tutoring. We can offer that."

The question had changed from "what will it take to fill up our Sunday morning children's programs?" to "how can we make a difference from Monday, Tuesday, Wednesday, Thursday and Friday?"

Limiting questions, on the other hand, might not be questions at all. They may only be thinly masking a statement of blame, obligation or guilt, e.g., why did you do it that way?

What makes a question powerful? Powerful questions are:

- Directly connected to deep listening, enabling the coach to craft the most effective question. Early on in my coaching, I believed there was only one right question. I would even equip myself with a long list of questions that I could scan while coaching. What I quickly discovered was that the most powerful questions were created in the moment, and the power of the question was directly related to my ability to listen deeply.
- Brief. They get right to the point. While it can be difficult to resist adding an explanation or another question, practice waiting for the person to respond.

> *John said, "I've got so many papers on my desk that I can't see the desk anymore. How can I get better organized?" Having coached John on and off for many years, I knew that organization was not his strength. I said, "John, let's not waste any time. We both know that organization is not your strong suit. Who can help you get better organized? And now that you're free of the need to be organized, what will be the best use of your time?"*

- Free of any hidden agenda. They are not leading or suggestive ("que-ggestions"). Powerful questions help the person or group being coached move further along the path of discovery.
- Usually open-ended, promoting further conversation. For the most part, yes/no questions usually result in a yes/no response, which force an end to the conversation and enable either/or

thinking. Powerful questions promote both/and thinking, opening the coachee up to a fuller range of possibilities.

- For the benefit of the one we are coaching. Remember that the coach is not the expert, and does not have to figure anything out or come up with solutions. Therefore, our questions must be designed to help the coachee discover and develop their own perspective and wisdom about the situation.

When I asked Pastor Julie the best use of our coaching call, she replied, "I'm exhausted and overwhelmed and I need a vacation. I'd like to take a big vacation every year and just get away – escape to somewhere where no one knows me and I'm out of cell and Internet range. I just need to rest and relax." During the course of our conversation, Julie recounted numerous past vacations and how wonderful they had been. She needed another one. We spent the bulk of the coaching call developing a plan based on the question, "How do I relax and rest in a big way this upcoming year?" With the plan in place, Julie had successfully met her goal for the call. Yet I sensed we weren't done. "So tell me, Julie, what are some little, daily getaways you can take for rest and relaxation?" She just laughed and then said "That's not possible. I have too much to do and too many people depending on me." At this point I observed, "Julie, you are good at designing big yearly getaways." I went on, "What's stopping you from designing daily mini getaways?"

Within minutes, Julie's eyes filled with tears and she said, "My father died a few years ago. He owned his own restaurant. He used to always say to us, 'Don't run the blender non-stop. You'll burn out the motor. If you turn it off every so often it will last much longer.'" Julie then picked up her mobile and said "I haven't been able to turn it off." After a long pause, Julie turned off her phone.

There are six types of powerful questions:

1. **Vision/Possibility Questions.** Questions that help the person to gain greater clarity about what is possible:

   - What does success look like?
   - What do you really, really want?
   - What's possible?
   - If we were sold out on what's possible, what would be possible?
   - What's the truth about this situation?
   - What's at stake?
   - What is past this issue?
   - Where is God in all of this?
   - What is God's invitation to you/us?
   - What are the signs that we're playing too small?
   - What's the bigger game?

2. **Concrete/Action Questions.** Questions that call for action:

   - What's next?
   - What can you do right now, today?
   - How soon can we have this resolved?
   - What's the first step?
   - What is the simplest next step?
   - What is the most outrageous next step you could take?
   - When will you take this first step?

- What needs immediate attention? Right now!
- What's the cost of not taking action?
- Who will do what by when?

3. **Curiosity/Thought-Provoking ("Hmm...") Questions.** Questions that help the person evoke discovery and create new awareness:

- What is the legacy that you want to leave behind?
- Where is sabotage showing up?
- What is the number one skill or behavior you need to master?
- What keeps you up at night?
- What is your relationship with money?
- What leap of faith do you need to take?
- In a nutshell, what's the real issue?
- What's on the back burner that needs to be placed on the front burner?
- What grades have you been handing out to others? Yourself?
- When has worry paid off for you?
- What if things are as bad as you say they are?

4. **Challenge/Reality Check Questions.** Questions that get to the heart of the issue and help create a much-needed shift in perspective or understanding:

- What is the truth about this situation?
- What's the best use of your time and energy today?
- What will you no longer tolerate?
- What will it take for you to become part of the solution?

15

- What rules or traditions do you have that keep getting in the way?
- What kinds of problems and crises do you keep attracting?
- What consumes your time to the point that it distracts you from attaining your goals?
- Where and when are you playing it safe?
- When are you most likely to become defensive?
- What are you pretending not to know?
- What's the cost of not changing?

It takes courage to challenge your clients and shift the conversation away from the direction they have requested.

In one case, I had been called in to coach a ministry team because the team seemed to be stuck and didn't know how to move forward. The goal for the one-day session was to help them understand why they were stuck. For the first part of the day, I observed the team as a whole and also spent individual time with each team member. The day wrapped up with a team meeting, when I shared my observations and did some group coaching.

I began the wrap-up by stating: "I know that I have been brought in to help you understand why you are stuck and I am prepared to offer you feedback about that. Before we do that, though, with your permission I would like to shift the question from, 'Why are we stuck?' to 'What steps can we take right now, today?'" They hemmed and hawed until I said, "Okay, let's have some fun. What if I told you that you couldn't go home today until each of you had identified one action step – it could even be the smallest of baby steps. What steps could you take right now?" They laughed and joked about not wanting to miss a basketball game on TV. Then they started to offer next steps. It wasn't too long until it really was time to end our meeting and go home. By then they had produced a 90-day plan, complete with action steps for each team member. By the way, we never did have time for their initial question, "Why are we stuck?"

5. **Acknowledgment Questions.** Questions that place us firmly in the moment and help us embrace who we are and what we've done:

   - What big or small wins are you tempted to overlook?
   - Who is your biggest fan?
   - If a spontaneous celebration erupted right now, what would you be celebrating?
   - What is perfect about today?
   - Who could you catch doing something right today?
   - What keeps you from seeing others as an "A+"?
   - What's great about you, and what's great about your church?
   - What are your favorite ways to celebrate?
   - What valuable role does celebration play in your forward progress?
   - What do you risk missing by not celebrating?

6. **God Questions.** Questions that center us and remind us of the Divine:

   - What is the spiritual practice that you are most committed to?

- What Biblical character do you most relate to? Which one would you like to most resemble?
- What keeps you from hearing the still small voice of the Divine?
- What are the best ways for you to experience the sacred each day?
- What would be different if you really, REALLY believed Psalm 139?
- When is it hardest for you to take John 3:16 personally?
- What is God's invitation to you today?
- Who or what helps you stay centered?
- How do you know when you are off-center?
- Who can help you with this?

Common challenges when asking powerful questions

Learning how to use powerful questions can be like asking a right-handed person to tie their right hand behind their back and only use their left hand – awkward, clumsy and difficult. Reframing involves a lot of unlearning. On the first day of their coach training, I often tell students, "Over the next several days of our coach training, never, never, ever, EVER under any circumstances, begin a question with the following: Do you…, Will you…, Can you…, Are you…, or Could you…" A touch dramatic, maybe, but it works!

In my 10+ years of offering coach training, I have observed that no matter how quickly new coaches grasp the idea of powerful questions, they struggle to apply them in actual situations. Here are three of the most common ways that new coaches dilute the power of their questions:

1. They ask closed questions.

This is such a hard habit to break. Yet, in most cases, the simple act of opening up a closed question increases its horsepower significantly. For example, a new coach today asked, "Do you have support people that can help you right now?" This question would be much more powerful if it was opened up as: Who are the support people who can help you right now? Or, how can you tap into the support of your family and friends?

Here's an exercise to help you stop asking closed questions. Ask to coach a friend or family member that you feel incredibly comfortable with. Request that every time you ask a closed question they simply respond by saying either "yes" or "no" and nothing else. The awkwardness and the silence that follows will help cure you of closed questions.

2. They stack their questions.

Have you ever noticed that news reporters and talk show hosts often ask one question after another when they're interviewing someone? I often feel for the person being interviewed, who is wondering which question to answer. The same thing happens with coaches. Strive to ask one single question, and then stop. Even if it isn't the best question or you feel the need to explain your question – don't! Let the person you are coaching ask for further explanation if they need to.

I will never forget a new coach, who really struggled with stacking his questions, and what finally helped him kick the habit. Since most of his coaching was done over the phone, he decided to take full advantage of his mute button. As soon as he asked a question, he would quickly hit the mute button on his phone. He could stack away, yet the person being coached couldn't hear a thing. He actually began laughing at himself, and quickly stopped the habit of stacking his questions.

3. They ask long, in-depth, expansive questions.

The most powerful questions are often the simplest and shortest of questions, only three or four words. For example: What's next? Who can help? What's most important?

As a new coach, I also struggled with powerful questioning. In fact, this might seem ridiculous, but I collected lots of powerful questions, typed them in big bold font – each on a single page – and taped them all around my office walls and ceiling. That way, I would always have plenty of powerful questions at hand.

Powerful questions from the scriptures

Perhaps the richest source of powerful questions is the scriptures themselves. For example, in Genesis 3:9, God asks the first powerful question of Adam and Eve saying, "Where are you?" (a Challenge/Reality Check question). Think about this. Why does an all-knowing God need to ask a question, when God already knows the answer? Why then did God ask this question of Adam and Eve? He asked for their own benefit, as well as for the benefit of the reader.

Here are some other powerful questions that God asks in the Old Testament:

- God asked Cain two questions in Genesis 4:6 and 4:9, "Why are you angry?" (a Curiosity/Thought-Provoking question) and "Where is Abel, your brother?" (a God question).

- God asks Moses, who is offering one excuse after another, "What is in your hand?" (a Curiosity/Thought-Provoking question).

- In the year that King Uzziah dies, God asks, "Whom shall I send?" (a Concrete/Action question) and "Who will go for us?" (Isaiah 6:8) (a God question).

Likewise, the New Testament also contains many powerful questions. As you read through the books of Matthew, Mark, Luke and John, you discover that Jesus was masterful in his use of questions.

Jesus used powerful questions with his disciples and with many of those he interacted with and healed. While there is a prescriptive side to Christianity, Jesus is not primarily prescriptive. Instead, his model was to elicit and draw forth.

My all-time favorite question that Jesus asked is found in John 5:6. Jesus sees the paralyzed man waiting for the waters of the pool of Bethsada to stir so that he could get in the healing waters first, and asks, "Do you want to get well?" (a Challenge/ Reality Check question). What a great question! In the man's response, he blames others for not putting him into the pool. Jesus follows his powerful question with a direct statement, telling the man to get up and walk. And he does.

Here is a sample of other questions that Jesus asked:

- When the disciples were in a boat in a terrible storm, Jesus asked, "Why are you afraid?" (Matthew 8:26) (a God question).

- When they were faced with feeding a crowd of over 5,000 people, he asked the disciples, "Where shall we buy bread for these people to eat?" (John 6:5) (a Vision question).

- When many of his other followers were abandoning him because of his message, he asked the 12 Disciples, "You do not want to leave too, do you?" (John 6:67) (a Challenge/ Reality Check question).

- He asked the woman caught in adultery, "Where are your accusers? Has no one condemned you?" (John 8:10) (a combination of an Acknowledgement question and a Curiosity/Thought-Provoking question).
- After teaching the crowds about how much God cares for them, he asked them, "Why do you worry about what you will eat and what you will wear?" (Matthew 6:31) (a God question).

- He asked the man whose blindness he had healed, "Do you believe in the Son of Man?" (John 9:35) (a combination of a Curiosity/Thought-Provoking question and a God question).

- When Peter made his claim that he would die for Jesus, Jesus asked, "Will you really lay down your life for me?" (John 13:38) (a combination of a Challenge/Reality Check question and a Concrete/ Action question). And then, after his resurrection, Jesus asked him, "Do you love me?" (John 21:17) (a Curiosity question).

- When Pilate asked Jesus, "Are you the king of the Jews?", Jesus replied with a question: "Is that your own idea, or did others talk to you about me?" (John 18:34) (a God question).

In the first section of this book, you read that history changed when a single question changed. And in the scriptures you see many examples of how a single question dramatically changed lives. Questions are the most powerful tool at our disposal. A powerful question, created out of deep listening, can change everything. Change the questions, change your church.

"Our deepest fear is that we are powerful beyond measure."
— Marianne Williamson

"It doesn't work to leap a 20-foot chasm in two 10-foot jumps."
– American Proverb

SECTION THREE

Do Your Questions Need Reframing?

At a recent coach training program, several of the students were struck by the potential value of a well-placed powerful question and were eager to try it out at their own churches. One pastor was excited about how "this is going to transform our church leadership meetings." Off they went, back to the real world, new skills in hand.

The following week, one by one, these new coaches came back into the class. Yet those bright, hopeful faces from the previous class were gone. Instead, we saw puzzled, bewildered and confused expressions. As we debriefed their experiences from the previous week, several students reported that when they tried out the powerful questioning techniques they had learned, their questions had fallen as flat as lead balloons. One pastor stated that after posing his powerful question, a board member actually responded, "Huh?"

Upon further discussion, what we discovered is that, while they believed they were asking powerful questions, some of their questions were too long or in-depth for their listeners to follow. Others had asked what they thought were open-ended questions, but which turned out to be closed questions in disguise.

Another group of pastors, who were all from the same church, had asked very strong powerful questions, yet they weren't relevant to the leadership team's agenda. "We were so focused on using powerful questions that we completely forgot to listen to what the team was talking about. No wonder they looked at us like we were from Mars or had two heads or something."

Powerful questioning is a skill that takes time to develop. The best way to start is to notice and examine the types of questions you're asking now. I suggest that people actually record themselves coaching – you can purchase a digital recorder, or use a memo recording application on your mobile phone.

If you're recording your client sessions, you must have the client's permission. You can cover this in the coaching agreement you create at the beginning of your relationship. I suggest you also record an introduction to each session that states your name, your client's name, the reason the call is being recorded, and a verbal agreement from your clients, e.g., "This is (coach's name), coaching (client's name) on (today's date). This call is being recorded for the purposes of the coach's training and development, and this recording will be heard by (e.g., the coach, the coach's mentor). (Client name), do you agree to this?"

Listening to your coaching recordings is one of the most effective ways to develop the skill of powerful questions. A further step to add to this exercise is to stop the tape every time you identify an unhelpful question (we'll get into some examples of unhelpful questions below). Then, give thought to a more effective question that you could have asked. I went through this exercise once per quarter for my first eight years as a coach. In fact, this exercise really helped prepare me for my Master Certified Coach credential exam.

Once you can analyze your own questioning habits and identify the types of unhelpful questions you may be asking, you'll be able to step back and reframe them into more powerful questions.

Stephen, the pastor of a very large church, hired me as his coach. His church had recently made several decisions that he was against and he felt like he was losing his influence as a leader. He wanted to figure out what he was doing wrong. During our initial coaching call I asked him to help me understand what was going on. He said, "There are so many elephants in the room, I don't even know where to begin." He was really distraught and had difficulty talking.

After a few minutes I made a request, "Stephen, as a starting point, what are some of the elephants in the room?" And he began naming the issues in the situation, what he had called elephants in the room, ending with, "What am I doing wrong?" I asked him to tell me more about that one. He said that this question had played in his head like a broken record throughout his life. And he recounted numerous difficult situations similar to the one he was currently in.

Midway through our coaching call I asked permission to ask a challenging question. He agreed and I asked the following, "Of all the elephants in the room that you mentioned, which one have you been giving the most attention and energy?" He quickly named the one, "What am I doing wrong?"

I then made a request. "I'd like you to step out of the room filled with elephants. Step out of the story and become an outside observer of this situation. Now, from outside of the room, which elephant really needs the most attention in order to best lead this church forward?" What followed was dead silence that spoke volumes. Almost immediately his whole demeanor changed and he said "This isn't about me.

I'm making it about me. But it's not about me." And then he listed the core issue at hand for his church and a plan of action began to evolve.

Here are seven types of unhelpful questions, along with sample questions that I've heard from pastors and churches.

1. Questions that are out of date.

I've heard the expression, "If 1955 ever returns, the Church will be incredibly ready." We are incredibly prepared for yesterday, but our questions are keeping us in the past. For example:

- How do we get them to come to us?
- How do we get them to be more like us?
- What kind of pastor do we need?

Reframe these into **Concrete/Action** questions.

2. Questions that let us stay asleep (Rip Van Winkle questions).

We miss things and sleep right through them, missing opportunities and other BFOs (blinding flashes of the obvious). It's like when your hand is right in front of your face but it's so close you can't tell it's your hand. These questions keep you caught in a time warp, so that even as you're waking up, you're still behind. For example:

- How do I escape?
- How do we get those who have left our church to come back?
- What can we do to feel really, really good about ourselves?

- How do we implement the changes that we really, really need to make without offending too many people?

Reframe these into **God** questions.

3. **Questions that let us off the hook.**

They make us feel okay about not doing what we know we need to do. They allow us to wallow in our excuses and stay comfortable. In fact, a friend of mine once referred to the church as "the cult of the comfortable." For example:

- Why can't we be more like the XYZ church?
- Why aren't the newer (younger) people stepping up?

Reframe these into **Challenge/Reality Check** questions.

4. **Questions that limit our perspective.**

They shut down the creative process, so instead of having a wide expanse of possibilities, we're left with just a little slice. While blinders can be helpful to limit distractions, most of the time they're just a hindrance. For example:

- How much longer can we afford a full-time pastor?
- What are we going to do?
- Why bother?

Reframe these into **Vision/Possibility** questions.

5. Questions that we've already answered before we ask them.

Leaders who ask these types of questions are the same ones who never delegate because they've already decided how everything is going to go. These are "que-ggestions," aimed to lead people exactly where you've decided they will go.

And just for fun, here is a list of some of the *least helpful* questions I've ever heard. They're all examples of questions that we've already answered before we ask them. If you've ever asked these, take heart and please keep reading. (These questions were contributed by Gary Crowell of the Tarrant Baptist Association in Ft. Worth, TX.)

- Why would you ever consider that possibility?
- Don't you feel you are making a bad mistake?
- Are you okay with not doing your best?
- How long is it going to take you to figure out what you want to do?
- Why do you seem incapable of arriving at a solution?
- How could you take such a misdirected course of action?

And my personal favorite: In what universe do you really, really think that your idea will work?

Reframe these into **Curiosity/Thought-Provoking** questions.

6. Questions that blind us to the truth.

People with visual impairment can sometimes see shapes and shadows, but not the whole picture. These kinds of questions stop our vision – literally and figuratively – of where we're going. For example:

- How do we get people to fund our budget?
- How do we care for our own people first?

Reframe these into **Vision/Possibility** questions.

7. **Questions that keep us moving at 90 miles per hour.**

We're in perpetual motion, never stopping, addicted to the next step, completely skipping over any sense of Sabbath or rest. For example:

- What are we going to do?

Reframe these into **Acknowledgement** questions.

So what's the harm in asking a few unhelpful questions? To illustrate this, I'll share the story of a church leadership team who made quite a bit of progress with reframing their questions, until ... well, read about what happened.

The danger of doubt – One church's story

"Everyone wants to be fixed, not many want to change."
– Myron Madden

More than a century ago, this church was formed when a group decided to break away from the mother church (10 miles away) to create a church that was closer and more convenient. Though the church was located in a fast growing and affluent area, no significant growth in membership had occurred for the past 50 years. Average attendance at Sunday worship has stayed at approximately 140 people. With the effects of downward attrition (people leaving or dying and no new members to replace them), their attendance numbers were starting to dwindle.

The church leadership prided themselves on traditions. Once a tradition is established, it continues year after year. For example, a singing group has visited the church to lead a service every year, twice a year, for the past 28 years.

While it has been very difficult to establish any new traditions, they tried something new by constructing a multi-million dollar multipurpose room and smaller rooms. This would serve as a meeting space for community organizations, as well as a large space to hold family and church events.

The problem was that, without new members and an increase in revenue, the church could not meet its financial obligations for the new multi-purpose room.

A few years ago, they had tried to address their membership goals by adding a second worship service – it was traditional, and practically identical to the current service. Their belief was that an additional service at a different time would attract new members. However, instead of attracting new members, the second identical service divided the attendance between two services.

No new people were being added.

In desperation, they hired a new pastor with expertise in contemporary, multi-media worship experience. They also hired a coach.

Very quickly the coach helped the church identify the primary question that governed and guided the majority of its decisions: What do we need to do to maintain what we already have? Variations included: What's best for us? How do we get them to join us?

The coach encouraged them to explore and brainstorm other questions; to reframe these questions into ones that were more powerful.

The key question that evolved was: "What step of faith can we take to have the biggest impact for God?"

What generated from this new question was the successful launch of a third worship service – very different from their other two worship services. Within four months, the combined worship attendance jumped to over 440 weekly and the numbers continued to increase for several years.

Unfortunately, about two and a half years into the process, the previous questions began to re-emerge. The long-term members panicked, noting that while the new service kept growing, the two traditional worship services were decreasing in numbers.

Several key leaders were focusing on the unhelpful question: When will these new people come over to our worship services and support us? This line of questioning spread like wildfire. Within 18 months the new pastor was gone and a new traditional pastor was hired with the mandate to build up attendance at the original two worship services.

Currently, the average attendance at all three worship services is about 110.

What heights do you think this church could have reached if they hadn't doubted themselves and reverted back to their old unhelpful questions?

SECTION FOUR

Success Stories – How These Churches Reframed Their Questions, and What Happened Next

Unlike the church in the previous example, the pastors and church leaders in these next stories were able to successfully transition to a culture of powerful questions. In the following section, I'll show you how to change YOUR questions and change your church.

Note: The names and other identifying details in these stories were changed to protect the anonymity of those involved.

Story #1: This country church needed to grow their mindset in order to grow their numbers.

"It is a terrible thing to look over your shoulder when you are trying to lead – and find no one there."
– Franklin D. Roosevelt

It was a small, country church (25-35 in attendance at Sunday morning worship) that for the past 150 years had been in a very rural part of the country. Over the past few years, a population boom has happened, which almost immediately changed the surroundings to suburbs. The church leadership saw this as their opportunity to grow, reach many more people and really make a difference in the community. While the change from rural to suburbs was dramatic, this faith community really wanted to embrace and welcome the new people that were moving into their local community.

They figured they'd use the same strategy that had worked for them for the past 150 years: Open the big red church doors and people would come. They went about sprucing up their church, i.e., painting, lawn care, a new sign, training members how to greet visitors, and creating a schedule of designated greeters for each Sunday morning. And to top it all off they put a fresh coat of red paint on the front church doors, along with a sign above that said "Welcome."

Then, they waited and waited – Sunday after Sunday – for new people to come. Only, no one came to visit. Well, maybe a few. But not near what they expected.

They became frustrated and morale was low. Their strategy wasn't working. Even worse, a new church opened up not too far from them and it was packed every Sunday.

They were asking unhelpful questions like these:

- *How do we get them (the new people) to come to us?*
- *Why would people rather go to church down the street?*
- *What's wrong with us?*

In their effort to address and answer these questions, they put up more welcome signs. They even posted a catchy slogan each week on their outside sign. They brought in a consultant to do a hospitality workshop and retrained all of the greeters and members.

Then, they hired a consultant to take them through a strategic planning process that resulted in the following three goals:

1. Start a new contemporary worship service.
2. Hire a youth pastor.
3. Upgrade the facility by adding air conditioning to the sanctuary.

They also hired a coach. And that's when things really started to change for the better. The coach met with the pastor and the church leaders, heard their questions and helped reframe them.

Instead of, *"How do we get the new people to come to us?"* They began to ask, *"What are the greatest needs of our new neighbors?"*

"Why would people rather go to church down the street?" turned into, *"How can we be most helpful to our new neighbors and respond to their needs?"*

Perhaps most importantly, *"What's wrong with us?"* became, *"What's great about us? What are our unique strengths and offerings?"*

Once the leadership team began asking how they could get to know their neighbors, they began brainstorming ways to get out into the community. They almost immediately began identifying easy ways to meet their new neighbors, e.g., they organized a welcome committee to take a basket to each new neighbor, personally welcome them and ask if they could be of any assistance.

Interestingly, the question about assistance produced the greatest results. Most of the new people to the neighborhood needed help with practical things, such as: *"Where's the nearest grocery store?"* *"What's the quickest way to get to the mall and avoid all of this traffic?"* *"Can you recommend a plumber, builder, doctor, etc.?"*

The challenge with this was that, while they were excited about meeting all their new neighbors, this didn't immediately translate into increased attendance on Sunday morning. What their new neighbors taught them over time was that what they really wanted in a church was different from what this once little country church was offering. For example:

Time of worship was important. They didn't want to go to an 11:15 a.m. Sunday worship service. Instead, most preferred 9:00 or 9:30 a.m.; that way they had the rest of the day to do other things. They also wanted something for their children at the same time as worship, NOT before or afterwards.

Most of the new neighbors had young children and they all wanted great programs for their children, e.g., nursery school and day care during the week, and a really great Sunday children's program, including a children's choir. For these people, the church nursery room was the most important room in the building – the comfort and safety of their children was key.

Reframing their questions and offering assistance to their neighbors produced several results for this church:

- The leadership team revisited their earlier strategic plan and factored in their newfound information about their neighbors.

- They set a goal of hiring a full-time children's pastor within three years.

- An official welcoming committee was formed and is still working.

- The leadership team helped the congregation to identify what was really great and unique about their church. For example, they identified that they really cared about other people, and meeting the practical needs of people was important to them.

- While they are still in the process of creating a contemporary worship service, what took precedence was launching several programs to meet local community needs, e.g., dinners for shut-ins over the holidays, a booklet listing neighborhood services and resources for their new neighbors, opening their facility to a local AA group, hosting the local blood drive and becoming a voter's site. Plans for a day care center are also underway.

- From a regular attendance averaging 25-35 worshippers, with the only growth from the birth of a new baby, at the time of this writing, average attendance has skyrocketed to 166 worshippers per week.

Story #2: When this church leadership team started listening, their congregants started talking.

"Listening is one of the greatest gifts you can give another person." – J. Val Hastings

From 1970 until about 2000, this was a rapidly growing church in a rapidly growing suburb. They prided themselves on being the place of worship that the corporate leaders of their community attend. Since the 1970s, their main – and highest attended – worship service has been very traditional and classical in nature.

Yet while their community was still growing rapidly, the church has not. From 2000 to 2007, they plateaued in terms of membership – any increases they saw with new members were cancelled out by those who left. By 2008, their membership, attendance and offerings had started to steadily decline.

In 2006, their long serving and dearly loved senior pastor retired. Their new senior pastor was doing well, but was not beloved like the former pastor.

The senior pastor and the leadership team couldn't quite articulate the core issue, but there was an overall uneasiness in the church and a sense that their best days were in the past, even though the local community continued to experience rapid growth.

The church leadership team, which included some of the community's top corporate leaders, all felt that some kind of intentional work with an outside expert was needed to turn this church around.

In the past, several outside consultants had been hired to help the leadership team develop a new vision and strategic plan. Additional outside experts were also brought in to administer assessment tools to help the leadership team diagnose what was wrong. Each of these attempts either stalled out, or were stopped because tension and conflict in the church seemed to increase.

Most of the leadership team had been working with their own coaches for many years and found the coaching process extremely helpful. They strongly urged their pastor to work with a coach. They were pleased to hear that their pastor had identified a coach that worked specifically with pastors and church leadership teams.

The senior pastor had two individual coaching sessions per month. There was also a two-hour group coaching session with the leadership team every other month.

The individual coaching sessions provided the senior pastor with a safe place to talk about how hard it was to follow a beloved senior pastor whom everyone revered. People acted like the former senior pastor walked on water.
On several occasions, the senior pastor expressed his frustration that people seemed to be in mourning over the retirement of the previous pastor and how long the process seemed to be taking. The actual death of the former pastor, which occurred during this process, felt like a major setback.

After about six months, the focus of the senior pastor's individual coaching sessions shifted into strategic conversations about how to move the congregation forward, how to establish himself as a leader and what his own legacy might be.

The group coaching with the leadership team provided opportunities for the lay leadership team to fully express what they were seeing and sensing. It also provided opportunities for many candid conversations between the pastor and leadership team. "Laying it all out on the table," as many referred to this process, felt both risky and helpful. Looking back, these candid conversations helped cement the relationship between the leadership team and the pastor and got them on the same page.

In both the individual and group coaching sessions, the coach did a lot of mirroring and "dancing in the moment," noting that it appeared as though a lot had been bottled up for years. So it was very important to provide a safe space for venting and candid sharing. This proved to be the best approach. In fact, the team was benefiting so much from this process that they looked for a way for the entire church to take part.

They established what they called "listening groups" for the entire congregation, beginning with a kick-off meeting that was facilitated by the coach. In addition to introducing and explaining the listening process, the coach also posed several questions to the large group.

One question proved very helpful: *"What are the 10 things that I, as your church coach, absolutely need to know about you as a church?"*

After several comments were shared, someone stated very angrily, *"The drums from that contemporary service are always right up there next to the altar and it keeps me from really worshiping during the main traditional worship service that I have always attended."* This triggered a whole series of similar comments.

After several comments, the coach interrupted and asked, *"What will it take to get past this issue?"*

Someone immediately stated, *"This has been going on since 1995, when the contemporary worship service was started. We felt like we couldn't speak up or say anything."* A few others made similar statements, and the coach probed further so he could better understand the issue.

What ensued, in both the large listening group and the smaller listening subgroups they broke into, was the clear identification of unresolved issues and conflict from the 1990s. Members who had joined or visited in more recent years stated that they definitely felt this low-grade tension and conflict during their initial visits to this church. It not only almost kept them from coming back, but they felt certain that it was keeping many others from attending and joining. Acknowledging this truth was a major turning point for this congregation.

The initial and ongoing listening groups have proved very beneficial for this church. The question shifted from, *"What's still bugging you about the past?"* to *"What's possible and desirable from here on out?"* Congregants and church leaders are talking, listening and dreaming together about the present and the future.

The contemporary worship service is now being held in their gymnasium, and it is now the church's largest worship service. More open dialogue by leadership and attendees has been intentionally scheduled. While the traditional worshippers wish their service were the larger one, they feel heard and engaged in the ongoing decisions of the larger church. Plans are in place to begin visioning and strategic planning in about a year.

The senior pastor continues to meet regularly with his coach, with the full support of the leadership team. And slowly, the senior pastor and the leadership team are adopting the belief that their best days are still ahead.

Story #3: This senior pastor had to look within to heal the conflict on his team.

"When two bull elephants fight, it is the grass that suffers."
– African Proverb

The senior pastor of a large, growing church needed help with an ongoing conflict between two paid staff. Highly regarded and respected by his staff and church members, the senior pastor had a direct and candid leadership style, never afraid to "pull any punches" or share his opinion. Yet, he had adopted a very indirect strategy in solving this dilemma. As a result, the conflict continued to escalate and was now affecting the large team and select parts of the congregation.

For example, he took the entire staff through a variety of training in hopes that the two staff members involved in the conflict would see their issue in a new light and resolve the conflict. They tried:

- Individual and team personality assessments
- Conflict training
- A laser tag, team-building retreat
- A leadership retreat for paid and non-paid leaders and staff, focused around the topic of resolving conflict and working together as a unified team

The senior pastor was approached by a new coach, who was looking for coaching clients as part of his training. During their initial coaching session, the coachee filled the coach in on the background of the two staff and what he had tried so far.

The second coaching session began with the senior pastor brainstorming ways to address the staff conflict. He was trying to answer the unhelpful question, *"What else can I do to solve this problem?"*

The coach noted that the senior pastor kept coming up with indirect solutions, similar to the ones that hadn't worked in the past. Then the coach asked the following powerful question: *"What is keeping you from being direct and candid in this situation and simply requesting that these two staff resolve this now?"*

This one question shifted the entire coaching conversation from focusing on the conflict between the two staff to a deep discussion about the senior pastor and how his own beliefs and assumptions were at work in this situation.

For example, one of his limiting beliefs was that a pastor should have an answer to every problem. Yet, in this conflict, the senior pastor was stumped and really didn't see any realistic solution to resolving this conflict.

Another layer to the story was that the senior pastor was related, by marriage, to one of the two staff members in question. He was trying his best to remain impartial, but he knew that no matter how the situation turned out, it would be a topic of conversation at family gatherings.

The senior pastor was also feeling an internal conflict. Because he was normally so direct about things, he felt like he wasn't being himself. He feared that if the conflict wasn't resolved soon, he would just "blow his stack," and he knew that expressing anger this way would not be appropriate.

Over the course of several coaching sessions, the senior pastor devised a plan that was true to him. This plan included:

- Putting boundaries in place to limit the discussion of ministry-related topics at home and at larger family gatherings.

- Scheduling a meeting with his relative and having a candid conversation about the distinction between their family and work relationship.

- Holding a meeting for both staff members with the simple direction that the two of them resolve the conflict immediately or else both would face disciplinary action.

After implementing the strategy, the two staff members resolved their conflict and the senior pastor was thrilled with the results. He continues to work with his coach, focusing mainly on setting boundaries, creating more family and personal time, and exploring additional ways to develop his leadership.

Story #4: From pastor to senior pastor – it was about time for a change.

"Before sunlight can shine through a window, the blinds must be raised." – American proverb

Ron has been a pastor for over 25 years. He takes tremendous pride in his pastoral care, citing that he will frequently visit longer than expected if needed, and that he will re-arrange his entire schedule at the last minute to visit and pray with a church member.

His previous churches had applauded and appreciated Ron's emphasis on pastoral care. While his current church appreciates his care for parishioners, they also want a pastor that is a leader. This church has several retired pastors who offer pastoral care, while their senior pastor has always been the one to cast vision, develop leaders and move the church forward.

Ron was finding it very difficult to let others take over the pastoral care. In fact, on several occasions he has missed or showed up late to leadership meetings because he was providing pastoral care to a parishioner – even though one of the retired pastors was already providing pastoral care.

The leadership team saw Ron's behavior as unprofessional. While most liked Ron as a person, they were not satisfied with him as a senior pastor.

When they insisted he let others take on the pastoral care, Ron was able to do that. He set up weekly meetings with the retired pastors so that he could stay involved and be in the loop.

Yet when it came to taking on a more visionary leadership role, team members continued to be dissatisfied with Ron and his leadership. Ron didn't understand. He felt that he was doing what they wanted, yet everyone seemed to be mad at him before he even entered the leadership meetings.

Ron was told that he had to work with a coach in order to develop his leadership skills. While Ron would not have sought out a coach on his own, he knew he needed help in leadership and was eager to start working with his coach.

Ron had two individual coaching sessions by telephone per month. Ron wanted to use the coaching times to develop his ability to cast vision and develop action plans for the church. He cited several books that he was reading and two leadership training events that he was planning on attending. Yet even though Ron tackled these books and applied the principles, very little improvement was noted by Ron or others.

The coach observed that Ron regularly showed up several minutes late for his scheduled coaching sessions and frequently went overtime. After several sessions, the coach addressed this behavior. Ron's flippant response was, *"Yeah, you sound like my wife. She's always telling me that I'm late and that I have no regard for people's time."* The coach asked, *"What's the truth about what your wife regularly tells you?"* Ron stated, *"That's just her. She gets mad because I'm always coming home later than expected. She's threatened to buy me a watch..."*

The coach intuited that something important was going on here, and followed up with this powerful question: *"Ron, what's the truth about you and time and your current leadership challenges at this church?"*

There was a long pause and then Ron said, *"Ah, I think I understand what's going on! It's not just about me doing too much pastoral care. I often get caught up in phone calls and roll into meetings a few minutes late. And worship never ends on time. You know, the spirit moves and I don't want to stop the spirit. But this is a Pennsylvania Dutch church and they value punctuality. In fact, they often laugh and say that if someone shows up on time at this church, then they are late! That's a big part of what's going on. So that's why they are mad at me!"*

Immediately, Ron began showing up early for all church-related events. People were pleasantly surprised by his early presence. Ron noted that the anger toward him dissipated almost immediately and the leaders related to him very differently.

Ron continued reading leadership books and implementing leadership principles. Except now they actually seemed to be working.

Ron continues to work with his coach. In fact, Ron has enrolled in coach training and is planning to adopt a coach approach to pastoring. His leadership team fully supports this plan of action.

Story #5: This multi-site church had to take a step back in order to move forward.

"If people can't see what God is doing, they stumble all over the place. But, when they attend to the things of God (see what God is doing) they are most blessed."
– Eugene Peterson translation of Proverbs 29:18

This large, and growing, suburban church had multiple sites and multiple staff. They offered a tremendous variety of worship and other ministry opportunities, which both their own community and the unchurched population found very appealing.

The staff and church leadership team worked regularly with coaches and consultants and found these external resource people to be very helpful. Four years ago, they underwent a major visioning process to develop a strategic plan for the following three years. Having implemented that three-year plan, they were ready to develop new next steps.

Overall, things seemed to be going well. They were growing in attendance, and it was obvious they were meeting needs in the local and global community.

Yet something felt "off" to the staff and leadership team. They identified that the issue was not having the next three years mapped out.

They tried to work on this several times on their own, but they seemed to get bogged down in the process. When they did come up with some steps, there was a feeling of unrest about them.

Since working with external resource people had worked well in the past, they brought in a coach to help. This particular coach had already worked with the church on several occasions for retreats and staff development training.

The coach was hired to spend the day with the staff and leadership team to develop next steps with them. For the first few hours, the coach asked questions and probed into what was going on with the team, for example:

- *Fill me in on the process up until now.*
- *What seems to be the core issue?*
- *Tell me more.*

Eventually, the discussion turned to their agenda for the day. When the coach asked the group what question or problem they wanted to solve, the unanimous response was, *"What are our next steps in our vision?"*

Then the coach asked the group's permission to reframe this question, and the group reluctantly agreed.

The coach then suggested that for the next 30 minutes or so that they work on answering this question:
"What are your beliefs about your vision?"

The responses were telling, and it was immediately clear that this question was at the core of the issue. While they were carrying out their previous strategic plan so beautifully, along the way their vision had changed; not completely, but enough to require re-visioning. That's why no matter how hard they had tried to develop next steps, nothing was going to work because their vision was off.

In that one day, with that one reframed question, this very capable leadership team took proactive steps to address the real issue and crystallize the new vision that had already been emerging. From there, a strategic plan fell naturally into place and they were off and running.

Story #6: An interim pastor asked, "How can the start be as powerful as the end?"

"Life is like a 10-speed bike. Most of us have gears we never use." –
Charles M. Schulz

The pastor in this story is an intentional interim pastor, and had been one for the past 20 years. She had successfully lead several churches through the change of pastors and helped them transition forward and grow their church.

She had just started with a new church and wanted to know the best way to lead her new interim pastorate. She felt that even though her previous positions always ended up well, she could be doing more to start out better. She was seeking both leadership development and practical help and support.

She had already read several books on leadership, and had spoken with many seasoned interim pastors to ask for their suggestions. After experiencing a coach training event, she decided to hire her own coach.

In their telephone coaching sessions, her coach listened deeply as the pastor described her situation and what she wanted. *"I know how to end well,"* she said, *"I trust the process and the leaders in the church. In fact, I'm a '10' with how things end up. But what additional training and resources do I need in order to lead well in the beginning?"*

Her coach took that question and helped her reframe it into one that was much more powerful:

"How can I show up as a "10," not only at the end, but from the beginning?"

This shift in question immediately produced an "aha" and helped her feel very positive about herself and her leadership effectiveness. Subsequent coaching conversations focused on how she could show up as a "10," including things like getting more sleep, scheduling intentional rest time between appointments, regular meditation, and positive reminders to trust herself as well as those she was pastoring.

These actions all helped to lower her feelings of stress, which in turn increased her own, and other people's, confidence in her leadership from the start. She felt *"empowered, not fixed,"* by this process, and exclaimed, *"I can't believe that it was in me all along!"* Best of all she genuinely believed that *"This new interim is going to be much more enjoyable than any others."*

Story #7: Maybe his team wasn't the problem after all.

Bill is the founder and senior pastor of a rapidly growing church. He has been at this church for the past 18 years. He currently has 22 full-time employees on his ministry team. He frequently describes his team as a family. It's not unusual for Bill to "go the extra mile" and bend the rules for individual members of his team, because he considers them to be his family. He finds it difficult to fire even the worst of the ministry staff, because he's really concerned about their welfare.

Bill's vision is to grow from a single site church to a multi-site ministry. He believes that he can do this within the next three to five years. In addition to implementing this multi-site vision, he would also like to spend less time at church and enjoy life more. His big dream is to take a year-long sabbatical and let the ministry run without him.

Bill created a strategic plan and action steps to move towards his goal, and he's making moderate progress. He is becoming very aware that his current ministry team is slowing things down. He is also frustrated that his "ministry family" doesn't share his enthusiasm for his vision. When Bill initially hired his coach, it was to help him implement the multi-site ministry plan. How could he empower and equip his ministry team to implement his plan of action?

After several coaching sessions, Bill expressed his frustration about his team's lack of enthusiastic action. Then he added, *"Maybe I'm the one that's holding back this vision. It feels like all the pieces are there, but maybe there's something that needs to change about me."*

At the encouragement of his coach, Bill continued to talk about this new discovery. After about 10 minutes, Bill said. *"You know, I really do need a sabbatical. I'm tired and worn out. While I love what we've done over the past 18 years, this has been hard work. Instead of talking about how to get my team to implement my plan, let's talk instead about getting me re-energized about ministry – by taking that sabbatical."*

At the time of this writing, Bill is away on his sabbatical – a combination of study, travel and relaxation.

·

SECTION FIVE

How to Reframe Your Questions and Change Your Church

Powerful questions are just one part of your church's overall visioning process. If you want to make real lasting change, I recommend these five steps:

1. Get out the Windex and clear up your view of where you/your team/your congregation are going.

Some say the journey of a thousand miles begins with the first step. I disagree. The journey of a thousand miles begins when you identify your destination.

If you were planning a trip to Alaska, you would need to make very different preparations and decisions than if you were planning a trip to Hawaii. Imagine how cold you'd be in your bathing suit!

My belief is that visioning is not nearly as complicated as what some people make it out to be. I've been doing vision work with people and organizations for 20 years, and what I see is that we don't create visions, we uncover them – and a single powerful question can make that happen. For example:

What do you really, really, REALLY want?

Check out the other Vision questions in Appendix C and find the ones that are a good fit for you and your team or community.

2. Listen deeply for the answers.

Powerful questions come directly out of deep listening – really listening deep and peeling the layers away, getting behind the surface to the platelets below. Before you even begin to craft a question, get deep and listen.

Deep listening is analogous to taking all of the pieces out of the puzzle box and laying them out – right side up, grouped in colors. Almost immediately you see things much clearer.

As she documented in her book, *Time to Think: Listening to Ignite the Human Mind*, Nancy Kline provided an opportunity for every member of a senior management team to listen and be listened to. The result reported was a time savings of 62%, which translated into 2,304 manager hours per year.

If we listen deeply enough, often the answers will pop right out. The ideal listening ratio for coaches is to be listening 80% of the time and responding 20% of the time. Did you know that words comprise only about 7% of what we communicate? That's right. The rest of our message is delivered with non-verbal cues, silence, tone of voice, quality of breath, etc. That's why coaches must listen at multiple levels, for example:

- Listen to what the other person is saying, as well as what they are not saying.
- Listen to what your own intuition tells you (gut-level listening).
- Listen without judgment, criticism or agenda (create a safe place for the person to share).
- Listen without thinking about what you will be saying next.
- Listen for values, frustrations, motivation and needs.

- Listen for the greatness in the person you are coaching.
- Listen for limiting beliefs and false assumptions.
- Listen for shoulds, oughts and musts (indicators of obligation and guilt).
- Listen for the obvious.
- Listen for the tone, pace, volume, inflection and frequently used words (also, notice when these change).
- Listen for the larger context.
- Listen attentively to the end of the statements (the best words often flow out last).

To be able to listen at multiple levels, a coach must quiet their mind of any mind chatter or internal conversations. They must create a physical environment that promotes deep listening, by attending to the space and pace of life and by managing their scheduling and calendar. Coaches grow to be comfortable with silence – resisting the urge to fill the space. As a new coach, a seasoned coach told me that deep listening is similar to standing in a pool. In order to see the bottom clearly, you must be still – absolutely still.

3. Ask helpful questions.

Be aware of your tendency to ask certain types of unhelpful questions, e.g., out of date questions. (Refer back to Section Three for the other types), so you can be on the lookout for when you repeat that pattern. Simple awareness can often be just the thing that jostles us into a new habit.

4. Identify your place in the problem-solving process.

Big Picture Stage. You're at one of those defining moments when a shift in focus and vision can yield tremendous results. You discover that you've been playing too small and there is a bigger game at stake. The "same old, same old" won't cut it anymore. You know at the core of your being that another way of being is called for and that the platelets beneath your church are shifting big time.

First Steps Stage. Momentum is needed. It's like steering a car. It's easiest to steer when the car is moving. At this stage you want to generate movement and momentum so that you can begin steering into the vision.

Motoring Along Stage. I liken this to cruise control while driving your car on a long trip. Cruise control allows you to maintain a steady pace/speed, which provides maximum gas mileage and distance achieved.

Abandonment Stage. You've been at this a while and your hope is waning. It's still possible to turn around and go back, and it's very tempting to do just this.

Leadership Succession Stage. Major leadership changes of individuals and teams are about to happen or have already occurred. Here's when the baton needs to be successfully passed to the next leaders without losing too much momentum.

Resistance/Plateau Stage. This is often the most vulnerable point in the journey. Though rest is needed, rest can be perceived as failure or possible failure. Naysayers often turn up the volume and say, "I told you so." The challenge is to catch your breath and regain momentum without stalling out or getting stuck. Also, new information can be gleaned by listening to the naysayers and their criticism. Golden nuggets of valuable truth for course corrections can be received.

Celebration Stage. It's time to acknowledge what has (and hasn't) happened. Both are needed: Let's applaud and acknowledge our accomplishments, and let's also apologize for missteps and mistakes along the way.

5. Open yourself up to more powerful questions.

Choose some from our lists in Section Two and Appendix C and try those on for size. As you get more comfortable with this style of questioning, you'll gravitate towards your favorites and find the ones that are most effective for your situation.

Creating a culture of powerful questions

Leading with questions is a whole new leadership model. If the leadership – ordained and non-ordained – is not sold on the case for leading with questions, you will never create an environment of powerful questions.

Gary, a reserved and quiet person, asked, "As an introvert, how can I get up the courage to stand up and boldly lead my church?" I asked Gary to tell me about some of the recent successes in his church, and who took the lead. He recounted time after time after time of a key church leader (non-ordained) taking the "bull by the horns" and making things happen.

After hearing several success stories I asked Gary what the common threads running through these successes were? Laity taking the lead was one common thread. He had great church members that were eager to do things. I asked about his role in these successes. He said "I met privately with each individual and helped them develop a plan. I encouraged them and became their person of accountability. I praised them publicly and was a cheerleader for their project."

Gary started out asking about how to change his leadership and personality style. By the end of the session, he was able to state this affirmation: "I am an introvert, already using my leadership and coaching skills to boldly lead my church forward."

This leadership model does not come naturally; training is needed. And with training comes practice, practice and more practice. As individuals and as a leadership team, use the resource lists of questions in the back of this book. Try them on, experiment, be willing to be unsure of yourself.

Accountability to this new approach is key, especially when resistance surfaces. Leaders can reinforce the new model by acknowledging and rewarding people for asking powerful questions. They also can and must provide regular opportunities for questions to be raised.

Even though many of the questions will be the "same old, same old" questions that may not be particularly helpful, this book gives you the skills to reframe them into powerful questions that will move your church forward.

As we've discussed, powerful questions are almost always open-ended and exploratory. You do not ask a powerful question if you already know the answer. So another key component to a culture of powerful questions is for leaders to be willing to go public with "not knowing."

In some cultures, leaders are seen as ineffective if they ask questions. "You're the leader, tell us what to do." Weaning your church from that mentality is a whole big shift right there.

Focus on baby steps and power through any resistance or setbacks. Empower yourself by having a plan in place ahead of time for how you will address resistance and setbacks.

Dealing with resistance

Resistance is inevitable. In fact, if resistance doesn't surface, you can't be sure any real, lasting or substantive change is underway.

In his book, *Managing Transitions*, William Bridges calls this the "marathon effect." Here's how it works: In the largest marathon events, a staggered start time is used to process the multitude of runners. By the time the last group starts the race, some of the first group will already be finishing.

When your church is going through a big change, you as the leader have likely started the change long before the rest of your community. You've been thinking about it, planning it and talking about it. When it's time to finally implement the change on a broad level, you're probably looking ahead to your next challenge.

So how do you handle conflict or tension in the people who are still new to the change? How do you handle resistance to your questions?

First of all, it helps if you expect withdrawal to occur. After all, most organizations have spent years in a "command and control" culture. They are used to leaders telling them what to do and doling out the answers, versus asking questions and inviting people into the process.

Also, be on the lookout for people who will use withdrawal as an opportunity to try and seize control. Instead, YOU can carpe diem – seize the day – by listening deeply and reframing questions in a way that keeps everyone together and moving forward towards your common vision.

Be willing to ask the honest questions, even in the face of skepticism and resistance: Are we ready to do what is really needed now? If not, what do we need to do to get ready?

Listen vigilantly to your own questions. Eliminate any disempowering questions and increase your empowering questions. This book shows you exactly how to do that.

Resist the urge to fix things or people. Instead of moving into problem-solving mode, stay in curiosity and listening mode longer. When you really hear the issues that people are raising, it's amazing what you can learn. Be visible and available. The more accessible you are, the more helpful a leader you can be.

Imagine how different things will be when the majority of church leaders, pastors, ministry staff and church leaders are actively reframing their questions and turning them into powerful, transformational questions.

In the first section of this book, I mentioned Anne Rice's July 2010 Facebook comment that she had quit being a Christian, reflecting many people's experiences of having lost faith in the church. With our new reframed questions, the next Facebook proclamation may be that "Anne Rice and thousands like her have returned to the church!"

Take the risk to launch a new culture of powerful questioning in your church. Go for it!

"One doesn't discover new lands without consenting to lose sight of the shore for a very long time."
– Andre Gide

APPENDIX A

How to Use the Resource Questions

If you're looking to develop your capacity for asking powerful questions, the best thing to do is practice, practice, practice.

The following sections give you three different ways to find questions that fit your particular situation.

For example, are you planning a spring retreat? Check out Appendix B for some April, May and June questions.

Are you bogged down by too many details? Look to the "Vision Questions" in Appendix C.

Has your team reached a plateau as you work towards your goals? Refer to Appendix D for questions that relate to that stage of the problem-solving process.

One way to submerge your team in powerful questions is to commit to read these sections together.

And be sure to have this book on hand during your team meetings. That way, at any moment someone can stop and say, "Wait, I think we could be asking a more powerful question here," then flip through the book and find one!

APPENDIX B

Resource Questions by Month – A Year of Questions

January

1. What's your definition of your best year ever?
2. What part of this upcoming year most troubles you?
3. What good financial habit could you put in place this year?
4. What part of this upcoming year is most exciting?
5. What part of the past year do you want to carry over into the New Year?
6. What do you absolutely need to leave in last year?
7. What did you learn this past year?
8. Who was your biggest fan this past year?
9. What's the best use of your time and energy in this upcoming year?
10. What is the number one skill or behavior you absolutely have to master in this upcoming year?
11. What will you no longer tolerate?
12. What actions can you take to silence your negative inner tapes?
13. What is the spiritual practice that you are most committed to?
14. What does an experience of God feel like?
15. What would dramatically increase your experience of God?
16. When has worrying paid off for you?
17. What is one thing you could do to drastically reduce worry?
18. What needs more attention, right now, today?
19. What needs less attention, right now, today?
20. What causes you to laugh out loud with rib-splitting laughter?
21. What habit of yours would you like to pass on to others?
22. What habit do you never, ever, under any circumstance, want to pass on to others?

23. What biblical character do you most relate to in the scriptures, and why?
24. What biblical character would you like to resemble, and why?
25. What would make today special for you?
26. If a spontaneous celebration erupted right now, what would you celebrate?
27. What do you most want from your family and friends?
28. If you were free of self-doubt, what would be different today?
29. What is your relationship with money?
30. What's going well for you right now?
31. What suggestions would you give someone who wants to have more fun?

February

1. Where and when are you playing it safe?
2. What is playing it safe costing you, and what is it costing others?
3. What are you learning about God so far this year?
4. What's your ripple effect?
5. What myth about yourself are you keeping alive?
6. How well do you deal with uncertainty?
7. What do you really believe about asking for help?
8. How can you take better care of yourself right now, today?
9. In what ways has God been generous to you?
10. What is most important for you to tackle today?
11. What's the inner tape you play when you find it hard to say "No"?
12. Who makes you jealous?
13. What are you learning about love?
14. What or who comes to mind when you think about love?
15. What's the most challenging part of love for you?
16. What's your definition of the perfect partner?

17. What would it take to rekindle love?
18. When are you most likely to become defensive?
19. What is your track record regarding love – really?
20. What steps can you take so that your words and actions match?
21. What does getting more organized mean to you?
22. How can you become part of the solution?
23. What tips would you give someone about really enjoying life?
24. What is your body trying to tell you?
25. What is absolutely perfect about today?
26. What will it take for you to feel refreshed and rested each day?
27. What do people who take really good care of themselves know?
28. What three ways could you deepen your experience of God?

March

1. What can you do to be more effective this month?
2. What's the one question that you need to be asking yourself this month?
3. What needs your immediate attention going forward this month?
4. What does your body need to thrive and be healthy?
5. What are you hanging on to that you could release?
6. What rules do you have that keep getting in the way?
7. How have you experienced God's abundant love today?
8. What new ways of being are needed for you to move forward?
9. What's the most wonderful thing about God?
10. What can you do to show that you really care?
11. What can you do to communicate more effectively?
12. How can you be a better friend?
13. If a friend were in a similar situation as you, what would you suggest?
14. What part of your life needs the powerful touch of God today?

15. What would it take to create the change that you want?
16. If success was a certainty, what next steps would you take?
17. What's taking shape? What's beginning to emerge?
18. What is your secret ambition?
19. What does your ideal living environment include?
20. Where have you been giving your power to others?
21. What would enough look like?
22. In a nutshell, what's the issue?
23. How do you add stress to your life and complicate things?
24. If you knew that people would follow your leadership, where would you be going?
25. What are you pretending not to know?
26. What's your favorite way of sabotaging yourself?
27. What do you want more of?
28. What do you want less of?
29. What keeps you from hearing the still small voice of the Divine?
30. What would cause you to jump with joy this week?
31. What more could you accomplish if you lowered your standards?

April

1. Who are you willing to trust with your hopes and dreams?
2. What would be different if you really, REALLY believed Psalm 139?
3. When is it hardest for you to take John 3:16 personally?
4. What new and creative ways has sabotage begun showing up?
5. What's your belief about money and how well is that currently serving you?
6. What pearls of wisdom have you been recently handing out to others?
7. What's not complete yet?

8. What's on the back burner that needs to be placed on the front burner?
9. How are you doing, really?
10. What is God inviting you to be a part of today?
11. What's the REAL problem?
12. What kind of person would you be if you were driven by passion?
13. What dream have you long since given up on?
14. What's the leap of faith you need to take?
15. Which of your roles could someone else be doing, and probably better than you?
16. What's the worst thing that could happen if you did less?
17. Why is it so much easier to plan than it is to take action?
18. What is the hardest part about delegating?
19. Who is someone you would love to have on your team, but you haven't asked yet?
20. Who do you know that regularly gets things done, and what can you learn from them?
21. Who makes you jealous?
22. If you really dared to dream big – really BIG – what would your life look like?
23. What can you hand off?
24. What's your most treasured memory of Easter?
25. What grades have you been handing out to others?
26. What grades have you been handing out to yourself?
27. What would be possible if you had a team?
28. How is being stuck serving you, and what is it costing you?
29. What if your assumptions are wrong?
30. Whose life are you living?

May

1. When do you enjoy others the most?
2. When do you enjoy yourself the most?
3. What do you really, REALLY want?
4. What's perfect about today?
5. What are you WAITING for?
6. What has changed the most so far for you this year?
7. What still needs to happen in order for this to be your best year ever?
8. What is your favorite phrase or saying? Why?
9. What or who gives you the courage to go on?
10. What are your beliefs about what you really, REALLY want?
11. What is only now beginning to unfold in your life?
12. What really empowers you?
13. What was your earliest experience of God?
14. How did you experience the overflow of God's love today?
15. For what do you most long for in your relationship with God?
16. Ecclesiastes 3:1-8 says there is a time for everything. What time is it for you right now?
17. Who can help you with what you really, REALLY want?
18. What was the best day of your life?
19. What is keeping you from having hope?
20. What do you want to be when you grow up?
21. What's the lie that you keep telling yourself?
22. What has to happen in order for you to be in "the zone"?
23. When is it hardest for you to say "No"?
24. What are those tasks that only you can do to receive what you really, REALLY want?
25. What action could you take to get rid of your negative inner tapes permanently?
26. What is your track record in life so far?

27. What is the greatest lesson you've learned?
28. If you gave up worrying, what would life be like?
29. What REALLY matters?
30. How would you know if you were in a disempowering relationship?
31. What have you outgrown?

June

1. What's your heart telling you?
2. What do you need to say goodbye to in order to move forward?
3. What is the decision you are avoiding?
4. What keeps you up at night?
5. What aren't you telling me that's keeping you stuck?
6. What healthy boundaries can you establish right now?
7. What ten things will you say "No" to today?
8. What makes your heart sing?
9. What is one thing you feel really good about from this past week?
10. What is the legacy that you want to leave behind?
11. What do you really believe about yourself?
12. What internal rules and unspoken standards are having a negative impact on you?
13. What beliefs and assumptions no longer serve you?
14. What would your life be like if you mustered the courage to do what you already know you need to do?
15. Who are the people that help you see the glass as half full, instead of half empty?
16. Who do you remind yourself of?
17. What's possible today?
18. What is God's dream for your life?

19. What kind of challenges and problems do you repeatedly attract?
20. What would life be like without anger?
21. Who can you forgive today?
22. What needs immediate attention, right now, today?
23. When was God most real to you today?
24. When are you most aware of God's amazing love for you?
25. What keeps you from experiencing God's amazing love for you?
26. Who or what is the source of most of your stress?
27. What are your healthy sources of energy?
28. What would make the biggest difference in your life today?
29. What would it take for you to treat yourself like your best friend?
30. What's working for you?

July

1. What kind of problems and crises do you keep attracting?
2. What do you continually do that limits your success?
3. What thoughts or messages are repeatedly playing in your head?
4. How much of a people pleaser are you?
5. What is God's deepest desire for you? Your Church?
6. What needs to be acknowledged that isn't being acknowledged?
7. What would you do differently if this problem were solved?
8. What has served you well in the past? Is it still serving you well?
9. What's the "should" in this situation?
10. Where would you like to grow your leadership in the next year?
11. How are you getting in your own way?
12. What would it take to catch people doing something right?
13. Are you owning your full potential?

14. What will you do to protect your priorities?
15. What are your fondest childhood memories of summer?
16. What new memories do you want to create this summer?
17. What will provide you with the greatest source of recreation during this season?
18. What will be the biggest benefits of play and recreation for you?
19. When is it hardest for you to play?
20. Who is your model of recreation and play?
21. What are you not saying?
22. What are your unhealthy sources of energy?
23. What's ahead?
24. What would make the biggest difference over the remaining months this year?
25. What would you do differently if there were no limits?
26. What are you pretending not to know?
27. What is the payoff of pretending not to know?
28. What will it take to be honest with yourself?
29. Who can best help you be honest with yourself?
30. What is the inner voice of your soul saying to you right now?
31. What are you most afraid of, and how might that fear be getting in the way?

August

1. What are the things that only you can do?
2. What are the things that you and others can do?
3. What are the things that you can do, but choose not to do?
4. What are the things that you cannot do and never want to do?
5. What new information have you gained from the previous four questions?
6. Based on the first four questions, what will you stop doing and delegate to someone else?

7. Based on the first four questions, how will your weekly schedule be different?
8. What has been the best part of this year so far?
9. What's still missing from this year?
10. What single step or action could you still take to make this your best year ever?
11. How could you use the next few weeks to prepare for this next season?
12. In what ways are you having the greatest impact in the lives of others?
13. What resources have you never used?
14. Where and when do you find the greatest meaning and purpose?
15. Where are your goals and purpose in conflict?
16. What is the simplest way to bring greater harmony between your goals and purpose?
17. How easy is it for you to say "I don't know"?
18. What are the true benefits of being able to easily say "I don't know"?
19. Who or what could help you with saying "I don't know"?
20. What are the best three things your favorite leader ever did?
21. What advice would your favorite leader offer you right now?
22. What gets you up and out of bed each morning?
23. What would happen if you did absolutely nothing today?
24. What are the real benefits of doing absolutely nothing on a regular basis?
25. What is the biggest challenge of doing absolutely nothing?
26. What are you doing well?
27. What are the positive qualities and ways of being that you bring to most tasks?
28. What new and creative qualities and ways of being would you like to add to your tasks?

29. What are you not doing that you really need to be doing?
30. What is the actual problem?
31. What gets in the way of you doing and being your best?

September

1. What's perfect about today?
2. What needs immediate attention, right now, today?
3. When was God most real to you today?
4. What's God up to?
5. When are you most aware of God's amazing love for you?
6. What keeps you from experiencing God's amazing love for you?
7. What do you want more of, and less of?
8. What are your healthy sources of energy?
9. What would make the biggest difference in your life today?
10. What is the true potential of your church?
11. What do you want the top three priorities of your pastor to be?
12. If you could change one thing about your church/ organization, what one thing would you change?
13. What makes you proud to be a part of your church/ organization?
14. What has to happen in order for your church/organization to be at its fullest potential?
15. When is your contribution to your church/ organization at its fullest potential?
16. What puts a smile on your face?
17. What role does contribution place in your life's purpose?
18. What are you committed to?
19. If not now, when?
20. What part of Psalm 23 is most important for you to hear today?
21. What is present when you learn best?
22. Who or what are you taking for granted?

23. When is it hardest for you to trust God, as we are invited to do in Proverbs 3:5-6?
24. On a scale of 1 to 10 (10 = total trust of God), what is your current trust level of God, and what would take it to the next level?
25. What part of God's responsibility are you feeling responsible for?
26. What are you tolerating today?
27. When would be a good time to stop tolerating so much?
28. Where are you overextending yourself?
29. When was the last time you clearly heard the still small voice of God?
30. What would it take to turn up the volume on the still small voice of God?

October

1. What's your heart telling you?
2. What do you need to say goodbye to in order to move forward?
3. What is the decision you are avoiding?
4. What is one simple thing you could do today to get you closer to your goal, right now, today?
5. What keeps you up at night?
6. What do you find yourself continually thinking about when you're lost in thought?
7. What are you tolerating?
8. What healthy boundaries can you establish right now?
9. What 10 things will you say "No" to today?
10. What has to happen in order to really involve others in your plans?
11. What is one thing you need to focus on to get where you want to go?

12. What are your reactions telling you about this situation?
13. What are the signs and signals that what you are pursuing no longer makes sense?
14. Are things as bad as you say they are, or are they worse?
15. What are five changes or actions that you can take in the next 30 days that will move you forward?
16. What consumes your time, to the point that it distracts you from attaining your goals?
17. How attached are you to the outcome?
18. What has you hooked?
19. What are the signs that your church is headed in the wrong direction?
20. What is your funniest experience in church?
21. What does your church stand for?
22. What are your greatest strengths?
23. Where are you falling down with follow through?
24. Where is self-sabotage showing up?
25. What is at the root of this conflict?
26. What are the action steps that only you can take today?
27. What is your most cherished memory?
28. What new cherished memories do you want to create?
29. What do you find most frustrating in life, and what's one thing you could do right now to address that frustration?
30. What is your real job description?
31. Who are the three leaders you most admire? Why?

November

1. Who are the individuals that have contributed the most to you, and what are the ways that you can acknowledge them today?
2. Who are you willing to trust with your hopes and dreams?

3. What would be different if you really, REALLY believed Psalm 139?
4. When is it hardest for you to take John 3:16 personally?
5. What new and creative ways has sabotage begun showing up?
6. What's your belief about money? How well is that currently serving you?
7. What pearls of wisdom have you been recently handing out to others?
8. What's not complete yet?
9. What's on the back burner that needs to be placed on the front burner?
10. What is beyond this problem?
11. When and how are you "should-ing" yourself? Others?
12. What in the world is God up to?
13. What is the one thing that you should never, ever, under any circumstances suggest that your team do?
14. What beliefs strengthen you?
15. At what point when you say "yes" are you really feeling like saying "no"?
16. What outreach can you provide that will impact thousands?
17. Based on an accurate review of your past three months, what are the top three areas where you have invested the most time and energy?
18. What frustrations are you ready to address?
19. What regularly distracts and discourages your leadership team?
20. Who is really in charge?
21. What makes your church unique?
22. What leadership lesson are you currently learning?
23. What is the rallying cry of your church?
24. What is the truth about this situation?
25. What's your most treasured memory of Thanksgiving?
26. What do you need from others right now?

27. What's missing?
28. What support do your key leaders need?
29. What are you going to do?
30. If chocolate is the answer, what's the question?

December

1. What does your soul need right now?
2. What are the signals that it's time to get started?
3. What legacy do you want to leave behind?
4. What brings your life joy?
5. What do you want to start doing?
6. What do you want to keep?
7. What's perfect about this season?
8. What are the best ways for you to experience the sacred each day?
9. How different would life be without defensiveness?
10. What has to happen for you to be free of long-standing anger?
11. Who contributed most to your success?
12. What other choices do you have?
13. What gifts do you have to share?
14. What does a great friendship look like?
15. What was missing for you this year?
16. What are you sowing?
17. What are you reaping?
18. How curious are you?
19. How do you learn best?
20. What or who always puts a smile on your face?
21. What or who inspires you?
22. What or who gives you courage during uncertain times?
23. Who can you catch today doing something right?
24. What would you like to be doing five years from now?

25. What will you commit to doing, and by when?
26. What limitations might you be placing on your dreaming and planning?
27. What suggestions do others continue to give you, yet you refuse to take?
28. What old belief system can you reprogram in the New Year?
29. In what area of your life do you want to have more fun?
30. If you had the ability to instantly change in the New Year, what would you change?
31. What key things still need to happen this year?

APPENDIX C

Resource Questions by Category

1. **Vision/Possibility Questions**

   a) What dream have you long since given up on?
   b) What's your definition of the big picture?
   c) In what ways are you playing too small right now?
   d) What's possible?
   e) What are you not seeing, and who can help you see bigger?
   f) How can your faith heritage play a more significant role in your vision?
   g) What do you really, REALLY want?
   h) What are your beliefs about what you really, REALLY want?
   i) Who can help you with what you really, REALLY want?
   j) What beliefs and assumptions no longer serve the BIG picture?
   k) What's not complete yet?
   l) What is only now beginning to unfold?
   m) What would be possible if you had a team?
   n) What is God's perspective of what is possible?
   o) What concerns you most about dreaming big?

2. **Concrete/Action Questions**

   a) What are those items that only you can do to accomplish what you really, REALLY want?
   b) What would you be doing if you mustered the courage to do what you already know you need to do?
   c) What is your full potential, and are you owning it?
   d) What steps can you take so that your words and actions match?

e) What rules do you have that are keeping you from getting started?

f) What new ways of being are needed for you to get started?

g) If a friend were in a similar situation as you, what would you suggest?

h) If success was a certainty, what next steps would you take?

i) If you knew that people would follow your leadership, where would you be going?

j) Why is it so much easier to plan than it is to take action?

k) What are you WAITING for?

l) What do you need to say goodbye to in order to move forward?

m) What decision are you avoiding that needs to be made?

n) What's possible today?

o) What would make the biggest difference today?

p) What is one simple thing you could do today to get you closer to your goal?

q) What will you commit to doing, and by when?

r) What is the number one skill or behavior you absolutely have to master in order to keep the momentum going?

s) What will you no longer tolerate?

t) What can you do to be more effective this month?

u) What is the one thing that you need to focus on to get where you want to go?

v) What does your next leader/leadership team absolutely need to learn from the current leader/leadership team?

w) What does your next leader/leadership team absolutely need to leave behind from the current leader/leadership team?

x) What habits or behaviors do you never, ever, under any circumstance want to pass on to the next generation of leaders?

y) What will it take to create the change that you want?

z) Who is someone you would love to have on your team, but you haven't asked yet? What will it take to invite them?

aa) What has to happen in order for you to be in "the zone"?

ab) What actions can you take to silence your negative inner tapes?

ac) What needs more attention, right now, today?

ad) What needs less attention, right now, today?

ae) What is most important for you to tackle today?

3. **Curiosity/Thought-Provoking Questions**

a) What's really possible?

b) If you really dared to dream big – really BIG – what would be different?

c) If your entire team and membership were sold on your big picture, what would be possible?

d) What's keeping you from being completely sold on your big picture?

e) What's the leap of faith you need to take?

f) Ecclesiastes 3:1-8 says there is a time for everything. What time is it for you and your church?

g) What's your heart telling you about the big picture?

h) Who are the biggest fans of your vision?

i) How can your biggest fans help you get started?

j) How might your biggest fans hinder your first steps?

k) Who or what really empowers you?

l) What's taking shape? What's beginning to emerge?

m) What are you pretending not to know?

n) When has worrying paid off for you?

o) What do you most want from others right now?

p) What myth are you keeping alive?

q) How well do you deal with uncertainty?

r) What do you really believe about asking for help?

s) What is your track record?

t) What are you most afraid of, and how might that fear be getting in the way?

u) As a leader, what's your ripple effect?

v) What tips would you give the next generation of leaders?

w) What pearls of wisdom have you been recently handing out to others?

x) Which of your roles could someone else be doing, and probably better than you?

y) What's the worst thing that could happen if you did less?

z) Who do you know that regularly gets things done? What can you learn from them?

aa) What can you hand off?

ab) What is the legacy that you want to leave behind?

ac) What kinds of challenges and problems do you repeatedly attract, and what will it take to break this attraction?

ad) What has served you well in the past? Is it still serving you well?

ae) Where would you like to grow your leadership in the next year?

af) What consumes your time, to the point that it distracts you from attaining your goals?

ag) What can you learn from your negative inner tapes?

ah) What's the inner tape you play when you find it hard to say "No"?

ai) When are you most likely to become defensive?

aj) How can you become part of the solution?

ak) What will it take for you to feel refreshed and rested?

al) What do people who take really good care of themselves know?

am) What can you do to show that you really care?

an) What have you outgrown?

ao) What keeps you up at night?

ap) Who makes you jealous?

aq) What are you learning about love?

ar) What or who comes to mind when you think about love?

as) What's the most challenging part of love for you?

at) What's your definition of the perfect partner?

au) What would it take to rekindle love?

av) What is your track record regarding love – really?

aw) What does getting more organized mean to you?

ax) What tips would you give someone about really enjoying life?

ay) What is your body trying to tell you?

az) How are you doing? Really?

ba) Who makes you jealous?

bb) What grades have you been handing out to others?

bc) What grades have you been handing out to yourself?

bd) Whose life are you living?

be) What do you want to be when you grow up?

bf) If you gave up worrying, what would life be like?

4. **Challenge/Reality Check Questions**

   a) What's the REAL issue?

   b) What is keeping you from having hope?

   c) What can you do to communicate more effectively?

   d) Where and when are you playing it safe?

   e) What is playing it safe costing you and others?

   f) What do you want more of?

g) What do you want less of?

h) What kind of person would you be if you were sold on the big picture?

i) What are you hanging on to that you could release?

j) What good financial habit could you put in place this year?

k) What's the best use of your time and energy at this stage?

l) What if your assumptions are wrong?

m) What or who are your healthy sources of energy, passion and conviction?

n) What part of this upcoming year most troubles you?

o) What's the one question that you need to be asking yourself and the larger leadership team?

p) What needs your immediate and full attention at this stage?

q) What's your belief about money, and how well is that currently serving you?

r) How will abandoning or jumping ship serve you, and how will it cost you?

s) What internal rules and unspoken standards are having a negative impact on you?

t) If you were free of doubt, what would be different today?

u) How can you take better care of yourself, right now, today?

v) In a nutshell, what's the issue?

w) What's your favorite way of sabotaging yourself?

x) What new and creative ways has sabotage begun showing up?

y) What's on the back burner that needs to be placed on the front burner?

z) What's the lie that you keep telling yourself?

aa) At this stage, what REALLY matters?

ab) What beliefs and assumptions no longer serve you?

ac) What do you continually do that limits your success?

ad) How much of a people pleaser are you?

ae) What would you do differently if there were no resistance right now?

af) What's past this resistance?

ag) How are you getting in your own way?

ah) What makes your wood wet?

ai) What will you do to protect your priorities?

aj) What do you really believe about yourself?

ak) How do you add stress to your life? Complicate things?

al) For the perfectionist: What more could you accomplish if you lowered your standards?

am) When is it hardest for you to say NO?

an) What healthy boundaries can you establish right now?

ao) What would life be like without anger?

ap) What if your assumptions are wrong?

aq) How different would life be without defensiveness?

5. **Acknowledgement Questions**

a) What or who inspires you?

b) What or who gives you the courage to go on?

c) Who are the people that help you see the glass as half full, instead of half empty (like Joshua and Caleb)?

d) What is most exciting, right now, today?

e) What causes you to laugh out loud with rib-splitting laughter?

f) What would make today special for you?

g) If a spontaneous celebration erupted right now, what would you celebrate?

h) What's going well for you right now?

i) What is absolutely perfect about today?

j) What would cause you to jump with joy this week?

k) What makes your heart sing?

l)   What long overdue apology will you make today?

m)   What's working for you?

n)   Who or what needs to be acknowledged that isn't being acknowledged?

o)   What is one thing you feel really good about?

p)   Who can you catch today doing something really great?

q)   What suggestions would you give someone about having more fun?

r)   What is one thing you feel really good about over this past week?

s)   Who can you forgive today?

t)   Who are the individuals who have contributed the most to you? What are the ways that you can acknowledge them today?

6. God Questions

a)   What's God up to?

b)   What's God already doing that you can join?

c)   What would the heroes of our faith say to us about our big picture?

d)   What would be different if you really, REALLY believed Psalm 139?

e)   What is God's invitation to you, right now, today?

f)   What are you learning about God on this journey?

g)   What would dramatically increase your experience of God throughout this process?

h)   What three ways could you deepen your experience of God?

i)   What keeps you from hearing the still small voice of the Divine?

j) What part of your life needs the powerful touch of God today?

k) In what ways has God been generous to you?

l) What biblical character do you most relate to in the scriptures, and why?

m) What biblical character would you like to resemble, and why?

n) How have you experienced God's abundant love today?

o) What's the most wonderful thing about God?

p) When is it hardest for you to take John 3:16 personally?

q) What was your earliest experience of God?

r) How did you experience the overflow of God's love today?

s) For what do you most long for in your relationship with God?

t) When was God most real to you today?

u) When are you most aware of God's amazing love for you?

v) What keeps you from experiencing God's amazing love for you?

w) What's your heart telling you?

x) What's the leap of faith you need to take?

y) What are the best ways for you to experience the sacred each day?

APPENDIX D

Resource Questions by Problem-Solving Stage

1. **Big Picture Stage Questions**

   a) What's God up to?
   b) What's God already doing that you can join?
   c) What's really possible?
   d) If our entire team and membership were sold on our big picture, what would be possible?
   e) What's keeping us from being completely sold on our big picture?
   f) What would the heroes of our faith say to us about our big picture?
   g) What's your definition of the big picture?
   h) Where and when are you playing it safe?
   i) What is playing it safe costing you and others?
   j) What do you want more of?
   k) What do you want less of?
   l) What would be different if you really, REALLY believed Psalm 139?
   m) What is God's invitation to you, right now, today?
   n) What kind of person would you be if you were sold on the big picture?
   o) What dream have you long since given up on?
   p) What's the leap of faith you need to take?
   q) If you really dared to dream big – really BIG – what would be different?
   r) What do you really, REALLY want?
   s) What are your beliefs about what you really, REALLY want?
   t) Who can help you with what you really, REALLY want?

u) What are those items that only you can do to accomplish what you really, REALLY want?

v) Ecclesiastes 3:1-8 says there is a time for everything. What time is it for you and your church?

w) What's your heart telling you about the big picture?

x) What would you be doing if you mustered the courage to do what you already know you need to do?

y) What is your full potential, and are you owning it?

z) What beliefs and assumptions no longer serve the BIG picture?

aa) What or who inspires you?

2. First Steps Stage Questions

a) Who are the biggest fans of your vision?

b) How can your biggest fans help you get started?

c) How might your biggest fans hinder your first steps?

d) What steps can you take so that your words and actions match?

e) What are you hanging on to that you could release?

f) What rules do you have that are keeping you from getting started?

g) What new ways of being are needed for you to get started?

h) If a friend were in a similar situation as you, what would you suggest?

i) If success was a certainty, what next steps would you take?

j) If you knew that people would follow your leadership, where would you be going?

k) Why is it so much easier to plan than it is to take action?

l) What are you WAITING for?

m) Who or what really empowers you?

n) What do you need to say goodbye to in order to move forward?
o) What is the decision that needs to be made to get started that you are avoiding?
p) What's possible today?
q) What would make the biggest difference today?
r) What is one simple thing you could do today to get you closer to your goal, right now, today?
s) What will you commit to doing, and by when?

3. **Motoring Along Stage Questions**

   a) What good financial habit could you put in place this year?
   b) What's the best use of your time and energy at this stage?
   c) What is the number one skill or behavior you absolutely have to master in order to keep the momentum going?
   d) What will you no longer tolerate?
   e) What are you learning about God on this journey?
   f) What can you do to be more effective this month?
   g) What's taking shape? What's beginning to emerge?
   h) What are you pretending not to know?
   i) What's not complete yet?
   j) What if your assumptions are wrong?
   k) What or who are your healthy sources of energy, passion and conviction?

4. **Abandonment Stage Questions**

   a) What part of this upcoming year most troubles you?
   b) What would dramatically increase your experience of God throughout this process?
   c) When has worrying paid off for you?
   d) What do you most want from others right now?

e) What myth are you keeping alive?

f) How well do you deal with uncertainty?

g) What do you really believe about asking for help?

h) What is your track record?

i) What three ways could you deepen your experience of God?

j) What's the one question that you need to be asking yourself, and the larger leadership team, at this stage?

k) What needs your immediate and full attention at this stage?

l) What keeps you from hearing the still small voice of the Divine?

m) What's your belief about money, and how well is that currently serving you?

n) What's the REAL issue?

o) How will abandoning or jumping ship serve you, and how will it cost you?

p) What or who gives you the courage to go on?

q) What is only now beginning to unfold?

r) What is keeping you from having hope?

s) What internal rules and unspoken standards are having a negative impact on you?

t) Who are the people that help you see the glass as half full, instead of half empty (like Joshua and Caleb)?

u) What is the one thing that you need to focus on to get where you want to go?

v) What are you most afraid of, and how might that fear be getting in the way?

5. Leadership Succession Stage Questions

a) What does your next leader/leadership team absolutely need to learn from the current leader/leadership team?

b) What does your next leader/leadership team absolutely need to leave behind from the current leader/leadership team?

c) What habits or behaviors do you never, ever, under any circumstance want to pass on to the next generation of leaders?

d) What habits and behaviors do you absolutely want to pass on to the next generation of leaders?

e) As a leader, what's your ripple effect?

f) What tips would you give the next generation of leaders?

g) What will it take to create the change that you want?

h) What pearls of wisdom have you recently been handing out to others?

i) Which of your roles could someone else be doing, and probably better than you?

j) What's the worst thing that could happen if you did less?

k) Who is someone you would love to have on your team, but you haven't asked yet?

l) Who do you know that regularly gets things done? What can you learn from them?

m) What can you hand off?

n) What would be possible if you had a team?

o) What has to happen in order for you to be "in the zone"?

p) What is the legacy that you want to leave behind?

q) What kind of challenges and problems do you repeatedly attract, and what will it take to break this attraction?

r) What has served you well in the past, and is it still serving you well?

s) Where would you like to grow your leadership in the next year?

t) What consumes your time, to the point that it distracts you from attaining your goals?

6. Resistance/Plateau Stage Questions

a) What actions can you take to silence your negative inner tapes?

b) What can you learn from your negative inner tapes?

c) What needs more attention, right now, today?

d) What needs less attention, right now, today?

e) If you were free of doubt, what would be different today?

f) How can you take better care of yourself, right now, today?

g) What is most important for you to tackle today?

h) What's the inner tape you play when you find it hard to say "No"?

i) When are you most likely to become defensive?

j) How can you become part of the solution?

k) What will it take for you to feel refreshed and rested?

l) What do people who take really good care of themselves know?

m) What can you do to show that you really care?

n) What part of your life needs the powerful touch of God today?

o) In a nutshell, what's the issue?

p) What's your favorite way of sabotaging yourself?

q) What new and creative ways has sabotage begun showing up?

r) What's on the back burner that needs to be placed on the front burner?

s) What's the lie that you keep telling yourself?

t) At this stage, what REALLY matters?

u) What have you outgrown?

v) What keeps you up at night?

w) What beliefs and assumptions no longer serve you?

x) What do you continually do that limits your success?

y) How much of a people pleaser are you?

z) What would you do differently if there were no resistance right now?

aa) What's past this resistance?

ab) How are you getting in your own way?

ac) What makes your wood wet?

ad) What will you do to protect your priorities?

ae) What do you really believe about yourself?

7. **Celebration Stage Questions**

a) What is most exciting, right now, today?

b) What causes you to laugh out loud with rib-splitting laughter?

c) What would make today special for you?

d) If a spontaneous celebration erupted right now, what would you celebrate?

e) What's going well for you right now?

f) In what ways has God been generous to you?

g) What is absolutely perfect about today?

h) What would cause you to jump with joy this week?

i) What makes your heart sing?

j) What long overdue apology will you make today?

k) What's working for you?

l) Who or what needs to be acknowledged that isn't being acknowledged?

m) What is one thing you feel really good about?

n) Who can you catch today doing something really great?

ABOUT THE AUTHOR

J. Val Hastings, MCC, is the Founder and President of Coaching4Clergy, which provides specialized training for pastors, church leaders and coaches. Val hired his first coach while he was pastoring at a local United Methodist church. His progress was noticeable by all, and he began to wonder, "What if I adopted a coaching approach to ministry? What if the larger church adopted a coaching approach to ministry?" In that moment, a vision began to emerge – a global vision of *Every Pastor, Ministry Staff and Church Leader a Coach.*

Val is the author of the book *The Next Great Awakening: How to Empower God's People with a Coach Approach to Ministry* and the e-book *The E3-Church: Empowered, Effective and Entrepreneurial Leadership That Will Keep Your Church Alive.* Val currently holds the designation of Master Certified Coach through the International Coach Federation, its highest coaching designation.